THE ROYAL HORTICULTURAL SOCIETY

DIARY 2002

Commentary by Brent Elliott

Illustrations from the
Royal Horticultural Society's Lindley Library

FRANCES LINCOLN

Frances Lincoln Limited
4 Torriano Mews
Torriano Avenue
London NW5 2RZ

The Royal Horticultural Society Diary 2002

British Library cataloguing-in-publication data
A catalogue record for this book is available from the British Library

ISBN 0-7112-1747-5

Printed in Hong Kong

First Frances Lincoln edition 2001

RHS FLOWER SHOWS 2002

All shows feature a wide range of floral exhibits staged by the nursery trade, with associated competitions reflecting seasonal changes and horticultural sundries. With the exception of the shows held at Malvern, Chelsea, Birmingham, Hampton Court Palace, Tatton Park and Wisley, all RHS Flower Shows will be held in one or both of the Society's Horticultural Halls in Greycoat Street and Vincent Square, Westminster, London SW1.

The dates given are correct at the time of going to press, but before you travel to a Show, we strongly advise you to check with the Diary Dates section of the RHS Journal *The Garden*, or telephone the 24-hour Flower Show Information Line (020 7649 1885) for the latest details.

FRONT COVER
A hand-coloured engraving of the hollyhock, *Althaea* or more correctly *Alcea rosea*, from the third volume of Ferdinand Vietz's *Icones Plantarum* (1806)

BACK COVER
A hand-coloured engraving of the sweet william, *Dianthus barbatus*, from the sixth volume of Ferdinand Vietz's *Icones Plantarum* (1817)

TITLE PAGE
A hand-coloured engraving of plants including crocus, centaurium, calendula and chicory, all contained in the first volume of Ferdinand Vietz's *Icones Plantarum* (1800), for which this was the title page illustration

OVERLEAF, RIGHT
A hand-coloured engraving of the musk mallow, *Malva moschata*, from the eighth volume of Ferdinand Vietz's *Icones Plantarum* (1818)

CALENDAR 2002

January

M	T	W	T	F	S	S
	1	2	3	4	5	6
7	8	9	10	11	12	13
14	15	16	17	18	19	20
21	22	23	24	25	26	27
28	29	30	31			

February

M	T	W	T	F	S	S
				1	2	3
4	5	6	7	8	9	10
11	12	13	14	15	16	17
18	19	20	21	22	23	24
25	26	27	28			

March

M	T	W	T	F	S	S
				1	2	3
4	5	6	7	8	9	10
11	12	13	14	15	16	17
18	19	20	21	22	23	24
25	26	27	28	29	30	31

April

M	T	W	T	F	S	S
1	2	3	4	5	6	7
8	9	10	11	12	13	14
15	16	17	18	19	20	21
22	23	24	25	26	27	28
29	30					

May

M	T	W	T	F	S	S
		1	2	3	4	5
6	7	8	9	10	11	12
13	14	15	16	17	18	19
20	21	22	23	24	25	26
27	28	29	30	31		

June

M	T	W	T	F	S	S
					1	2
3	4	5	6	7	8	9
10	11	12	13	14	15	16
17	18	19	20	21	22	23
24	25	26	27	28	29	30

July

M	T	W	T	F	S	S
1	2	3	4	5	6	7
8	9	10	11	12	13	14
15	16	17	18	19	20	21
22	23	24	25	26	27	28
29	30	31				

August

M	T	W	T	F	S	S
			1	2	3	4
5	6	7	8	9	10	11
12	13	14	15	16	17	18
19	20	21	22	23	24	25
26	27	28	29	30	31	

September

M	T	W	T	F	S	S
						1
2	3	4	5	6	7	8
9	10	11	12	13	14	15
16	17	18	19	20	21	22
23	24	25	26	27	28	29
30						

October

M	T	W	T	F	S	S
	1	2	3	4	5	6
7	8	9	10	11	12	13
14	15	16	17	18	19	20
21	22	23	24	25	26	27
28	29	30	31			

November

M	T	W	T	F	S	S
				1	2	3
4	5	6	7	8	9	10
11	12	13	14	15	16	17
18	19	20	21	22	23	24
25	26	27	28	29	30	

December

M	T	W	T	F	S	S
						1
2	3	4	5	6	7	8
9	10	11	12	13	14	15
16	17	18	19	20	21	22
23	24	25	26	27	28	29
30	31					

CALENDAR 2003

January

M	T	W	T	F	S	S
		1	2	3	4	5
6	7	8	9	10	11	12
13	14	15	16	17	18	19
20	21	22	23	24	25	26
27	28	29	30	31		

February

M	T	W	T	F	S	S
					1	2
3	4	5	6	7	8	9
10	11	12	13	14	15	16
17	18	19	20	21	22	23
24	25	26	27	28		

March

M	T	W	T	F	S	S
					1	2
3	4	5	6	7	8	9
10	11	12	13	14	15	16
17	18	19	20	21	22	23
24	25	26	27	28	29	30
31						

April

M	T	W	T	F	S	S
	1	2	3	4	5	6
7	8	9	10	11	12	13
14	15	16	17	18	19	20
21	22	23	24	25	26	27
28	29	30				

May

M	T	W	T	F	S	S
			1	2	3	4
5	6	7	8	9	10	11
12	13	14	15	16	17	18
19	20	21	22	23	24	25
26	27	28	29	30	31	

June

M	T	W	T	F	S	S
						1
2	3	4	5	6	7	8
9	10	11	12	13	14	15
16	17	18	19	20	21	22
23	24	25	26	27	28	29
30						

July

M	T	W	T	F	S	S
	1	2	3	4	5	6
7	8	9	10	11	12	13
14	15	16	17	18	19	20
21	22	23	24	25	26	27
28	29	30	31			

August

M	T	W	T	F	S	S
				1	2	3
4	5	6	7	8	9	10
11	12	13	14	15	16	17
18	19	20	21	22	23	24
25	26	27	28	29	30	31

September

M	T	W	T	F	S	S
1	2	3	4	5	6	7
8	9	10	11	12	13	14
15	16	17	18	19	20	21
22	23	24	25	26	27	28
29	30					

October

M	T	W	T	F	S	S
		1	2	3	4	5
6	7	8	9	10	11	12
13	14	15	16	17	18	19
20	21	22	23	24	25	26
27	28	29	30	31		

November

M	T	W	T	F	S	S
					1	2
3	4	5	6	7	8	9
10	11	12	13	14	15	16
17	18	19	20	21	22	23
24	25	26	27	28	29	30

December

M	T	W	T	F	S	S
1	2	3	4	5	6	7
8	9	10	11	12	13	14
15	16	17	18	19	20	21
22	23	24	25	26	27	28
29	30	31				

INTRODUCTION

The Renaissance tradition of the herbal died out in the eighteenth century, to be replaced by books on medical botany, often compiled by physicians rather than botanists. Plants were chosen on the basis of their role in *materia medica* (medicinal substances, whether animal, vegetable or mineral, used in the treatment of disease). These substances were usually dried specimens or crushed or powdered extracts, from which infusions could be prepared. Training in *materia medica* was part of a doctor's normal education and the larger hospitals often had their own gardens for growing the plants a physician would need to use. The illustrations in this diary are taken from two such books on medical botany by William Woodville and Ferdinand Vietz.

William Woodville (1752–1805) became physician to the Smallpox Hospital at Battle Bridge in 1791. Here he created a two-acre garden of medicinal plants within the grounds of the hospital, which was later swept away by the development of King's Cross station. From 1790 to 1793 he published his *Medical Botany* in three volumes (with a supplement in 1794), in which he described all the plants in the *materia medica* catalogues of the Royal Colleges of Physicians. The plates are unsigned, but his prospectus indicates that James Sowerby (1757–1822), a prominent botanical artist, both drew and engraved them. A second edition appeared in 1810, and in 1832 William Jackson Hooker, later the first Director of the Royal Botanic Gardens, Kew, revised the work for a third edition. It remained the standard English work on the subject until the 1870s.

Ferdinand Bernhard Vietz (1772–1815) was Professor of Medicine at the University of Vienna from 1801 to 1812 and then Director of the University Veterinary School until his death. His major work bore the cumbersome title of *Icones Plantarum Medico-Oeconomico-Technologicarum* (pictures of medical, economic and industrial plants). The first two volumes appeared in 1800 and 1804, with the plants arranged alphabetically. He then began to work more systematically, and in 1806 issued the first of several further volumes to include plants which had not appeared in volumes one and two. This third volume incorporated plants listed alphabetically, from *Acanthus* to *Amygdalus*. After Vietz's death, Joseph L. Kerndl undertook the task of editing the remaining unpublished work. The materials must have been fairly well advanced because volumes four to ten (*Anacardium* to *Zostera*) appeared in three years, from 1817 to 1819. Finally, in 1822, Kerndl issued an eleventh, supplementary volume with a further 100 plates.

Altogether, including the supplementary volume, Vietz's work included 1035 engravings. The artist and engraver was Ignaz Albrecht or Alberti, a Viennese artist whose dates are usually given as *fl.*1780–1801, on the basis of his entry in the great German dictionary of artists by Thieme and Becker, who concluded from the lack of references to him after 1801 that he must have died about then. However it seems likely that Vietz would have commissioned additional illustrations after the first two volumes were published and the order of plates suggests that they could not have been completed until well after 1804; and there is no evidence that other artists were involved in *Icones Plantarum*.

Brent Elliott
The Royal Horticultural Society

December ◊ January

31 Monday

1 Tuesday

New Year's Day
Holiday, UK, Republic of Ireland, Canada, USA, Australia and New Zealand

2 Wednesday

Holiday, Scotland and New Zealand

3 Thursday

4 Friday

5 Saturday

6 Sunday

Last Quarter

Epiphany

A hand-coloured engraving of the Christmas rose, *Helleborus niger*, drawn and engraved by James Sowerby, from the first volume of William Woodville's *Medical Botany* (1790)

January

WEEK 2

Monday 7

Tuesday 8

Wednesday 9

Thursday 10

Friday 11

Saturday 12

Sunday 13

New Moon

A hand-coloured engraving of the Seville orange, *Citrus aurantium*, from the first volume of Ferdinand Vietz's *Icones Plantarum* (1800)

January

WEEK 3

14 Monday

15 Tuesday

16 Wednesday

17 Thursday

18 Friday

19 Saturday

20 Sunday

A hand-coloured engraving of the saffron crocus, *Crocus sativus*, drawn and engraved by James Sowerby, from the third volume of William Woodville's *Medical Botany* (1793)

January

WEEK 4

Monday 21

First Quarter

Holiday, USA (Martin Luther King's birthday)

Tuesday 22

RHS London Flower Show

Wednesday 23

RHS London Flower Show

Thursday 24

Friday 25

Saturday 26

Sunday 27

A hand-coloured engraving of the almond, *Prunus dulcis* (formerly *Amygdalus communis*), drawn and engraved by James Sowerby, from the second volume of William Woodville's *Medical Botany* (1792)

January ◊ February

WEEK 5

28 Monday

Full Moon

Holiday, Australia (Australia Day)

29 Tuesday

30 Wednesday

31 Thursday

1 Friday

2 Saturday

3 Sunday

A hand-coloured engraving of the oxlip, *Primula elatior*, from the ninth volume of Ferdinand Vietz's *Icones Plantarum* (1819)

February

WEEK 6

Monday 4

Last Quarter

Tuesday 5

Wednesday 6

Holiday, New Zealand (Waitangi Day)

Thursday 7

Friday 8

Saturday 9

Sunday 10

A hand-coloured engraving of the pineapple, *Ananas comosus* (formerly *Bromelia ananas*), from the fourth volume of Ferdinand Vietz's *Icones Plantarum* (1817)

February

11 Monday

12 Tuesday

New Moon

Chinese New Year
Holiday, USA (Lincoln's birthday)
Shrove Tuesday

13 Wednesday

Ash Wednesday

14 Thursday

St Valentine's Day

15 Friday

16 Saturday

17 Sunday

A hand-coloured engraving of the snakeshead fritillary, *Fritillaria meleagris*, from the sixth volume of Ferdinand Vietz's *Icones Plantarum* (1817)

March

WEEK 10

Monday 4

Tuesday 5

Wednesday 6

Last Quarter

Thursday 7

Friday 8

Saturday 9

Sunday 10

Mothering Sunday, UK

A hand-coloured engraving of the sweet violet, *Viola odorata*, drawn and engraved by James Sowerby, from the second volume of William Woodville's *Medical Botany* (1792)

March

WEEK 11

11 Monday

Commonwealth Day

12 Tuesday

RHS London Flower Show

13 Wednesday

RHS London Flower Show

14 Thursday

New Moon

15 Friday

Islamic New Year (subject to sighting of the moon)

16 Saturday

RHS London Orchid Show

17 Sunday

St Patrick's Day
RHS London Orchid Show

A hand-coloured engraving of the quince, *Cydonia oblonga*, drawn and engraved by James Sowerby, from the second volume of William Woodville's *Medical Botany* (1792)

March

WEEK 12

Monday 18

Holiday, Northern Ireland and Republic of Ireland

Tuesday 19

Wednesday 20

Vernal Equinox

Thursday 21

First Quarter

Friday 22

Saturday 23

Sunday 24

Palm Sunday

A hand-coloured engraving of *Hepatica nobilis* (formerly *Anemone hepatica*), from the fourth volume of Ferdinand Vietz's *Icones Plantarum* (1817)

March

WEEK 13

25 Monday

26 Tuesday

27 Wednesday

28 Thursday

Full Moon

Maundy Thursday
Passover (Pesach), First Day

29 Friday

Good Friday
Holiday, UK, Republic of Ireland, Canada, Australia and New Zealand

30 Saturday

31 Sunday

Easter Sunday
British Summer Time begins

A hand-coloured engraving of the white or Madonna lily, *Lilium candidum*, drawn and engraved by James Sowerby, from the second volume of William Woodville's *Medical Botany* (1792)

April

WEEK 14

Monday 1

Easter Monday
Holiday, UK (exc. Scotland), Republic of Ireland, Canada, Australia and New Zealand

Tuesday 2

Wednesday 3

Passover (Pesach), Seventh Day

Thursday 4

Last Quarter

Passover (Pesach), Eighth Day

Friday 5

Saturday 6

Sunday 7

A hand-coloured engraving of the lilac, *Syringa vulgaris*,
from the tenth volume of Ferdinand Vietz's *Icones Plantarum* (1819)

April

WEEK 15

8 Monday

9 Tuesday

RHS London Flower Show

10 Wednesday

RHS London Flower Show

11 Thursday

12 Friday

New Moon

13 Saturday

14 Sunday

A hand-coloured engraving of *Tulipa gesneriana*,
from the tenth volume of Ferdinand Vietz's *Icones Plantarum* (1819)

April

WEEK 16

Monday 15

Tuesday 16

Wednesday 17

Thursday 18

Friday 19

Saturday 20

First Quarter

Sunday 21

Birthday of Queen Elizabeth II

A hand-coloured engraving of the dandelion, *Taraxacum officinale*, drawn and engraved by James Sowerby, from the first volume of William Woodville's *Medical Botany* (1790)

April

WEEK 17

22 Monday

23 Tuesday

St George's Day
RHS London Flower Show

24 Wednesday

RHS London Flower Show

25 Thursday

Holiday, Australia and New Zealand
(Anzac Day)

26 Friday

27 Saturday

Full Moon

28 Sunday

A hand-coloured engraving of the yellow flag iris, *Iris germanica*, from the seventh volume of Ferdinand Vietz's *Icones Plantarum* (1818)

April ◊ May

WEEK 18

Monday 29

Tuesday 30

Wednesday 1

Thursday 2

Friday 3

Saturday 4

Last Quarter

Sunday 5

A hand-coloured engraving of the opium poppy, *Papaver rhoeas*,
from the eighth volume of Ferdinand Vietz's *Icones Plantarum* (1818)

May

WEEK 19

6 Monday

May Day Holiday, UK (exc. Scotland) and Republic of Ireland
early May Bank Holiday, Scotland

7 Tuesday

8 Wednesday

9 Thursday

Ascension Day

10 Friday

Malvern Spring Gardening Show

11 Saturday

Malvern Spring Gardening Show

12 Sunday

New Moon

Mother's Day, Australia, Canada, New Zealand and USA
Malvern Spring Gardening Show

A hand-coloured engraving of *Rosa centifolia*, drawn and engraved by James Sowerby, from the third volume of William Woodville's *Medical Botany* (1793)

May

WEEK 20

Monday 13

Tuesday 14

Wednesday 15

Thursday 16

Friday 17

Jewish Feast of Weeks (Shavuot)

Saturday 18

First Quarter

Sunday 19

Whit Sunday (Pentecost)

A hand-coloured engraving of the flag iris, *Iris florentina*, drawn and engraved by James Sowerby, from the first volume of William Woodville's *Medical Botany* (1790)

May

WEEK 21

20 Monday

Holiday, Canada (Victoria Day)

21 Tuesday

Chelsea Flower Show

22 Wednesday

Chelsea Flower Show

23 Thursday

Chelsea Flower Show

24 Friday

Chelsea Flower Show

25 Saturday

26 Sunday

Full Moon

Trinity Sunday

A hand-coloured engraving of a clove pink, *Dianthus caryophyllus*, drawn and engraved by James Sowerby, from the second volume of William Woodville's *Medical Botany* (1792)

May ◊ June

WEEK 22

Monday 27

Holiday, USA (Memorial Day)

Tuesday 28

Wednesday 29

Thursday 30

Corpus Christi

Friday 31

Saturday 1

Sunday 2

A hand-coloured engraving of the mountain laurel, *Kalmia latifolia*, from the seventh volume of Ferdinand Vietz's *Icones Plantarum* (1818)

June

WEEK 23

3 Monday

Last Quarter

Golden Jubilee Bank Holiday, UK
Holiday, Republic of Ireland
Holiday, New Zealand (The Queen's birthday)

4 Tuesday

Bank Holiday, UK

5 Wednesday

6 Thursday

7 Friday

8 Saturday

The Queen's official birthday (subject to confirmation)

9 Sunday

A hand-coloured engraving of the stavesacre, *Delphinium staphisagria*, drawn and engraved by James Sowerby, from the third volume of William Woodville's *Medical Botany* (1793)

June

WEEK 24

Monday 10

New Moon

Holiday, Australia (The Queen's birthday)

Tuesday 11

Wednesday 12

Thursday 13

Friday 14

Saturday 15

Sunday 16

Father's Day, UK, Canada and USA

A hand-coloured engraving of *Fragaria chiloensis*,
from the sixth volume of Ferdinand Vietz's *Icones Plantarum* (1817)

June

WEEK 25

17 Monday

18 Tuesday

First Quarter

19 Wednesday

BBC Gardeners' World Live, Birmingham

20 Thursday

BBC Gardeners' World Live, Birmingham

21 Friday

Summer Solstice
BBC Gardeners' World Live, Birmingham

22 Saturday

BBC Gardeners' World Live, Birmingham

23 Sunday

BBC Gardeners' World Live, Birmingham

A hand-coloured engraving of chicory, *Cichorium intybus*, from the second volume of Ferdinand Vietz's *Icones Plantarum* (1804)

June

WEEK 26

Monday 24

Full Moon

Tuesday 25

Wednesday 26

Thursday 27

Friday 28

Saturday 29

Sunday 30

A hand-coloured engraving of the rock-rose, *Cistus creticus*, drawn and engraved by James Sowerby, from the second volume of William Woodville's *Medical Botany* (1792)

July

WEEK 27

1 Monday

Canada Day

2 Tuesday

Last Quarter

Hampton Court Palace Flower Show

3 Wednesday

Hampton Court Palace Flower Show

4 Thursday

Holiday, USA (Independence Day)
Hampton Court Palace Flower Show

5 Friday

Hampton Court Palace Flower Show

6 Saturday

Hampton Court Palace Flower Show

7 Sunday

Hampton Court Palace Flower Show

A hand-coloured engraving of *Angelica sativa* (now *Angelica archangelica*), from the first volume of Ferdinand Vietz's *Icones Plantarum* (1800)

July

WEEK 28

Monday 8

Tuesday 9

Wednesday 10

New Moon

Thursday 11

Friday 12

Holiday, Northern Ireland (Battle of the Boyne)

Saturday 13

Sunday 14

A hand-coloured engraving of a cultivated aconite or wolfsbane, *Aconitum × cammarum*, from the third volume of Ferdinand Vietz's *Icones Plantarum* (1806)

July

WEEK 29

15 Monday

St Swithin's Day

16 Tuesday

17 Wednesday

First Quarter

The RHS Flower Show at Tatton Park

18 Thursday

The RHS Flower Show at Tatton Park

19 Friday

The RHS Flower Show at Tatton Park

20 Saturday

The RHS Flower Show at Tatton Park

21 Sunday

The RHS Flower Show at Tatton Park

A hand-coloured engraving of dittany, *Dictamnus albus*, from the first volume of Ferdinand Vietz's *Icones Plantarum* (1800)

July

WEEK 30

Monday 22

Tuesday 23

Wednesday 24

Full Moon

Thursday 25

Friday 26

Saturday 27

Sunday 28

A hand-coloured engraving of the redcurrant, *Ribes rubrum*, drawn and engraved by James Sowerby, from the second volume of William Woodville's *Medical Botany* (1792)

July ◊ August

WEEK 31

29 Monday

30 Tuesday

31 Wednesday

1 Thursday

Last Quarter

2 Friday

3 Saturday

4 Sunday

A hand-coloured engraving of the jalap, *Ipomoea purga*, drawn and engraved by James Sowerby, from the first volume of William Woodville's *Medical Botany* (1790), where it was depicted under the name *Convolvulus jalapa*

August

WEEK 32

Monday 5

Summer Holiday, Scotland
Holiday, Republic of Ireland

Tuesday 6

Wednesday 7

Thursday 8

New Moon

Friday 9

Saturday 10

Sunday 11

A hand-coloured engraving of the sunflower, *Helianthus annuus*, from the seventh volume of Ferdinand Vietz's *Icones Plantarum* (1818)

August

WEEK 33

12 Monday

13 Tuesday

14 Wednesday

15 Thursday

First Quarter

16 Friday

17 Saturday

18 Sunday

A hand-coloured engraving of the common mallow, *Malva sylvestris*, drawn and engraved by James Sowerby, from the first volume of William Woodville's *Medical Botany* (1790)

August

WEEK 34

Monday 19

Tuesday 20

Wednesday 21

Thursday 22

Full Moon

Friday 23

Saturday 24

Sunday 25

A hand-coloured engraving of dittany, *Origanum dictamnus*,
from the eighth volume of Ferdinand Vietz's *Icones Plantarum* (1818)

August ◊ September

WEEK 35

26 Monday

Summer Holiday, UK (exc. Scotland)

27 Tuesday

28 Wednesday

29 Thursday

30 Friday

31 Saturday

Last Quarter

1 Sunday

A hand-coloured engraving of the cardoon, *Cynara cardunculus*, from the sixth volume of Ferdinand Vietz's *Icones Plantarum* (1817)

September

WEEK 36

Monday 2

Holiday, Canada (Labour Day) and USA (Labor Day)

Tuesday 3

Wednesday 4

Thursday 5

Friday 6

Saturday 7

New Moon

Jewish New Year (Rosh Hashanah)

Sunday 8

A hand-coloured engraving of a species of St John's wort, *Hypericum perforatum*, from the first volume of Ferdinand Vietz's *Icones Plantarum* (1800)

September

WEEK 37

9 Monday

10 Tuesday

11 Wednesday

12 Thursday

13 Friday

First Quarter

14 Saturday

15 Sunday

A hand-coloured engraving of the Turk's cap lily, *Lilium martagon*, from the seventh volume of Ferdinand Vietz's *Icones Plantarum* (1818)

September

WEEK 38

Monday 16

Jewish Day of Atonement (Yom Kippur)

Tuesday 17

RHS Great Autumn Show

Wednesday 18

RHS Great Autumn Show

Thursday 19

Friday 20

Saturday 21

Full Moon

Jewish Festival of Tabernacles (Succoth), First Day

Sunday 22

A hand-coloured engraving of a cone flower, *Echinacea purpurea*,
from the ninth volume of Ferdinand Vietz's *Icones Plantarum* (1819)

September

WEEK 39

23 Monday

Autumnal Equinox

24 Tuesday

25 Wednesday

26 Thursday

27 Friday

28 Saturday

Jewish Festival of Tabernacles (Succoth), Eighth Day
Malvern Autumn Garden and Country Show

29 Sunday

Last Quarter

Michaelmas Day
Malvern Autumn Garden and Country Show

A hand-coloured engraving of the common mulberry, *Morus nigra*, drawn and engraved by James Sowerby, from the second volume of William Woodville's *Medical Botany* (1792)

September ◊ October

WEEK 40

Monday 30

Tuesday 1

Wednesday 2

Thursday 3

Friday 4

Saturday 5

Sunday 6

New Moon

A hand-coloured engraving of hortensia, *Hydrangea macrophylla*, from the eleventh or supplementary volume of Ferdinand Vietz's *Icones Plantarum* (1822)

October

WEEK 41

7 Monday

8 Tuesday

RHS London Flower Show

9 Wednesday

RHS London Flower Show

10 Thursday

11 Friday

12 Saturday

13 Sunday

First Quarter

A hand-coloured engraving of purslane, *Portulaca oleracea*, from the ninth volume of Ferdinand Vietz's *Icones Plantarum* (1819)

October

WEEK 42

Monday 14

Holiday, Canada (Thanksgiving Day)
Holiday, USA (Columbus Day)

Tuesday 15

Wednesday 16

Thursday 17

Friday 18

Saturday 19

Sunday 20

A hand-coloured engraving of the common grape, *Vitis vinifera*, from the tenth volume of Ferdinand Vietz's *Icones Plantarum* (1819)

October

WEEK 43

21 Monday

Full Moon

22 Tuesday

23 Wednesday

24 Thursday

United Nations Day

25 Friday

26 Saturday

27 Sunday

British Summer Time ends

A hand-coloured engraving of the nasturtium, *Tropaeolum majus*,
from the supplementary volume of William Woodville's *Medical Botany* (1794)

October ◊ November

WEEK 44

Monday 28

Holiday, New Zealand (Labour Day)
Holiday, Republic of Ireland

Tuesday 29

Last Quarter

Wednesday 30

Thursday 31

Hallowe'en

Friday 1

All Saints' Day

Saturday 2

Sunday 3

A hand-coloured engraving of the China aster, *Callistephus* (formerly *Aster*) *chinensis*, from the fourth volume of Ferdinand Vietz's *Icones Plantarum* (1817)

November

WEEK 45

4 Monday

New Moon

5 Tuesday

Guy Fawkes' Day

6 Wednesday

First Day of Ramadān (subject to sighting of the moon)

7 Thursday

8 Friday

9 Saturday

10 Sunday

Remembrance Sunday, UK

A hand-coloured engraving of anise, *Pimpinella anisum*,
from the first volume of Ferdinand Vietz's *Icones Plantarum* (1800)

November

WEEK 46

Monday 11

First Quarter

Remembrance Day, Canada
Veterans' Day, USA

Tuesday 12

Wednesday 13

Thursday 14

Friday 15

Saturday 16

Sunday 17

A hand-coloured engraving of sugar cane, *Saccharum officinarum*, drawn and engraved by James Sowerby, from the third volume of William Woodville's *Medical Botany* (1793)

November

WEEK 47

18 Monday

19 Tuesday

RHS London Flower Show

20 Wednesday

Full Moon

RHS London Flower Show

21 Thursday

22 Friday

23 Saturday

24 Sunday

A hand-coloured engraving of the trumpet vine, *Campsis radicans*, from the fourth volume of Ferdinand Vietz's *Icones Plantarum* (1817), where it was depicted under the name *Bignonia radicans*

November ◊ December

WEEK 48

Monday 25

Tuesday 26

Wednesday 27

Last Quarter

Thursday 28

Holiday, USA (Thanksgiving Day)

Friday 29

Saturday 30

St Andrew's Day
Jewish Festival of Chanukah, First Day

Sunday 1

Advent Sunday

A hand-coloured engraving of the pear, *Pyrus communis*,
from the ninth volume of Ferdinand Vietz's *Icones Plantarum* (1819)

December

WEEK 49

2 Monday

3 Tuesday

4 Wednesday

New Moon

5 Thursday

6 Friday

7 Saturday

Jewish Festival of Chanukah, Eighth Day

8 Sunday

A hand-coloured engraving of bergamot, *Monarda didyma*, from the eleventh or supplementary volume of Ferdinand Vietz's *Icones Plantarum* (1822)

December

WEEK 50

Monday 9

Tuesday 10

Wednesday 11

First Quarter

Thursday 12

Friday 13

Saturday 14

Sunday 15

A hand-coloured engraving of capers, *Capparis spinosa*, from the fifth volume of Ferdinand Vietz's *Icones Plantarum* (1817)

December

WEEK 51

16 Monday

17 Tuesday

18 Wednesday

19 Thursday

Full Moon

20 Friday

21 Saturday

22 Sunday

Winter Solstice

A hand-coloured engraving of the Surinam quassia wood, *Quassia amara*, drawn and engraved by James Sowerby, from the second volume of William Woodville's *Medical Botany* (1792)

December

WEEK 52

Monday 23

Tuesday 24

Christmas Eve

Wednesday 25

Christmas Day
Holiday, UK, Republic of Ireland, Canada, USA, Australia and New Zealand

Thursday 26

Boxing Day (St Stephen's Day)
Holiday, UK, Republic of Ireland, Canada, Australia and New Zealand

Friday 27

Last Quarter

Saturday 28

Sunday 29

A hand-coloured engraving of mistletoe, *Viscum album*,
from the tenth volume of Ferdinand Vietz's *Icones Plantarum* (1819)

December ◊ January

WEEK 1, 2003

30 Monday

31 Tuesday

1 Wednesday

New Year's Day
Holiday, UK, Republic of Ireland, Canada, USA, Australia and New Zealand

2 Thursday

New Moon
Holiday, Scotland and New Zealand

3 Friday

4 Saturday

5 Sunday

A hand-coloured engraving of a daylily, *Hemerocallis fulva*, from the seventh volume of Ferdinand Vietz's *Icones Plantarum* (1818)

European National Holidays 2002

Holidays that fall on a Sunday are not included

AUSTRIA	Jan. 1; April 1; May 1, 9, 20, 30; Aug. 15; Oct. 26; Nov. 1; Dec. 25, 26
BELGIUM	Jan. 1; April 1; May 1, 9, 20; Aug 15; Nov. 1, 2, 11; Dec. 25, 26
DENMARK	Jan. 1; Mar. 28, 29; April 1, 26; May 9, 20; June 5; Dec. 24, 25, 26
FINLAND	Jan. 1; Mar. 29; April 1; May 1, 9; June 22; Nov. 2; Dec. 6, 25, 26
FRANCE	Jan. 1; April 1; May 1, 8, 9, 20; Aug, 15; Nov. 1, 11; Dec. 25
GERMANY	Jan. 1; Mar. 29; April 1; May 1, 9, 20; Aug. 15; Oct. 3; Nov. 1; Dec. 25, 26
GREECE	Jan. 1; Mar. 18, 25; May 1, 3, 6; June 24; Aug. 15; Oct. 28; Dec. 25, 26
ITALY	Jan. 1; April 1, 25; May 1; Aug. 15; Nov. 1; Dec. 25, 26
LUXEMBOURG	Jan. 1; April 1; May 1, 9, 20; Aug. 15; Nov. 11; Dec. 25, 26
NETHERLANDS	Jan. 1; Mar. 29; April 1, 30; May 9, 20; Dec. 25, 26
NORWAY	Jan. 1; Mar. 28, 29; April 1; May 1, 9, 17, 20; Dec. 25, 26
PORTUGAL	Jan. 1; Feb. 12; Mar. 28, 29; April 1, 25; May 1, 30; June 10; Aug. 15; Oct. 5; Nov. 1; Dec. 24, 25
SPAIN	Jan. 1; Mar. 29; May 1; Aug. 15; Oct. 12; Nov. 1; Dec. 6, 25
SWEDEN	Jan. 1; Mar. 29; April 1; May. 1, 9, 20; June 22; Nov. 2; Dec. 25, 26
SWITZERLAND	Jan. 1, 2; Mar. 29; April 1; May 9, 20; Aug. 1; Dec. 25, 26